I CAN SEE

Russ

Foreword

I got into writing through song lyrics. At no point did I consider myself a poet. Armed with a bass guitar and surrounded by like-minded pals, I put down lines that turned into songs. Gradually the lines got longer and turned into short stories, then scripts, then novels. Three novels, five albums and one collection of short stories later, I have finally got round to publishing a book of what I suppose could loosely be described as poetry, thanks to those beautiful souls at Wild Pressed Books.

Most of the words herein were originally featured on the three electronic/spoken word albums I helped to make with the legendary musician and producer Steve Cobby - *"My People Come From The Sea"*, *"Boothferry"* and *"Pound Shop Communism"*. The rest of the work has been accumulated over the years from fragments of songs and stories and notes to self, some of which were extended and finished and feature elsewhere in my other books. I suppose the common thread to everything I write is music, whether that be beats and noises captured on record or the music trapped forever in my head. I still don't consider myself a poet, but I hope anyone who loves poetry as much as I do enjoys the pictures these words create and finds some joy and beauty, some spark of recognition to light up the dark.

Love as ever to my family and friends and all the great writers and readers I've met down the years in the prisons, hostels, schools, retreats and community groups. Shine on.

Russ Litten, KUH, 2019.

These words are dedicated to Simon Bristow, the Prince of Print.

Contents

THE BOOKIE

Bring your offerings to my altar
like ransom notes from the future,
gnawed over, pored over,
names carved in blue,
charms to stop the universe
running away from you.

Pull in the reins, get it slapped down
then prostrate yourself before the HD screen,
shuffling slippers, bent spines, bad spleens
feeding chunks of gold into upright machines
like a wall of coffins gulping down life
and spitting back promises typed out and then
turned back into gold and stuffed in again.

But hope springs eternal when the day is most bleak,
when starting bells ring and whistles shriek
and for one brief and glorious second
you're singing an optimist song
where you live in the space
where you're not yet right
but you're not yet useless and wrong,
where time stands still and all bets are off
and the kids aren't hungry and the bills are paid
and the world hasn't got you by the balls
and you're soaring above the battlements
and the suffocating stench
of the sick pay walls.

Hold onto that feeling my friend,
hold it as tight as a betting slip,
and keep passing me the paper
that keeps me sweet,
in the safest job in an unsafe street.

ICELAND

There's a single Mam chatting to herself in Iceland,
she's got a snowstorm in her head and a gas fire in her gut,
it's a red-letter day in England,
the year of our Ham-Faced Overlord 2015
and the pressure is mounting,
that fridge in the kitchen back home has run out of magnets
and the final demands are dropping like extras in a cheap
      western,
meanwhile, our heroine is on auto-pilot,
doing what she can – don't let them in love,
the television does not own you
and that ringtone is an invitation, not a command –
the wolf-man is hammering down the door, don't let him in,
paint lasts longer than skin, she's plotting escape in her
      pippin
take me back to Tenerife, Flamingo Land, Berlin,
take us all away on an all-inclusive Caribbean holiday
take me anywhere, I don't care, just give me some paper
with the Queen's head on it and stamp my pass,
lay me down to sleep, put me out to grass,
just get me out of Iceland, intact,
but they're cranking up the pressure
and she can't ignore the adverts any longer, only ten more
sleeps till Christmas and it's getting dark outside,
but in the frozen wastes of Iceland
the overhead electric white strip lights
make everything look petrified –
imitation lobster tails, 4.99, prawn rings, two for one,
cardboard day-glo stars twinkle at every turn,
you cannot leave it on the shelf,
she only ever goes grafting when she's by herself,
Vienetta ice-cream in five fantastic flavours,
fill your boots before they're gone, dissolved, melted away,

2

like the resolve she left the house with,
like the wreckless dreams she once entertained,
for her and Bugger Lugs and Little Legs
and Tiny McSmall Fry
and that useless six foot two bastard who took to the hills
at the first sign of hardship,
the first heady whiff of shite, the ever-turning screw of life,
all them things kept tight inside,
all the things you do without,
like a living wage, like proper tampons,
like any form of sweet release,
like that hairdressing course at college,
the knowledge that your dreams
are a puddle of mint choc chip
and it's 2:34 pm in England,
the land of Our Sweet Lord 2015
and the planet turns it's face away from the sun,
stares out into the pitch black abyss of winter,
2:34pm, soon be time to get the bains from school,
and she's Young Mother Hubbard,
the cupboards are so bare they are barely there,
prehistoric caves, receptacles for malt vinegar and mouse
        droppings,
that burning gas fire below
and the snow-storm on the top deck;
there's not much time, she can't afford another fine,
nevertheless, she knows where the cameras are
and there's only two muppets on the till –
she knows the drill; turn your back on the magic eye,
hit the blind spot,
BANG!
crinkle-cut oven chips and ten economy burgers
slid marsupial style into the depths of the anorak,
the snowstorm in her head is now a raging blizzard,
but she maintains enough presence of mind
to make a perfunctory purchase

in order to slip past the gates of Iceland
without arousing suspicion,
the cardboard stars are talking to her,
will it be the spring roll and samosa party pack assortment
or the two-litre bottle of electric blue pop?
the basket bumps its way to the stone faced sentries
and it's a red-letter day in England
at the bone shuddering cold tail end of the year,
the year of Our Saviour 2015,
but Jesus has averted his eyes,
they are heavy, too heavy with suffering,
too many knock-off pills:
Valium, Diazepam, Temazepam,
don't fall asleep baby Jesus,
save us all, please, please, yeah, that'll be
four pounds seventy please,
dig around for sheckles,
the last bits of scraped-together silver,
do you want a receipt?
no thanks, see you later,
the last gasp chance, the final hurdle before another night
        tucked in,
the wolf-men kept away,
but just as she steps beyond the border
she feels a hand on her shoulder
– *can I just have a look in that bag please love?*

IN DEFENCE OF THE MOON

Do not blame my client the Moon
for all the lunatics walking the streets;
the actions of a few score maddened minds
are in no way due
to 81 billion tonnes of deadened rock
hung up in the sky above you.
Granted, the tidal pull may cause
fish to back pedal
and shore lines to settle,
but Armstrong's flag is not a red rag
to a gang of marauding mentals;
while they were wielding their kitchen knives
my client was waxing and waning
in some Tin Pan Alley tune,
or smiling down on lovers
as they embraced in a Mills and Boon.
Do not blame the Moon
for your carbon-based shortcomings.
You are all made of stars;
you will all receive a summons.

THE WINE-DARK SEA AND ME

Tricked the wind again today, hit the rope and whipped the
        flag, sent me on my way,
sent me on my merry way, sent me far away, the wine-dark
        sea, the wine-dark sea and me,
caught my death again today, lift the axe and tilt the mast,
        chip the ice away,
chip the blocks of ice away,
chase jack frost away, the tight drum skin of horizon and
        lands unseen, the wine-dark sea and me,

slept beneath the black of night, sail up anchor down,
        fastened to the sea by lights,
planets from the past alight, the wine-dark sea and me,
a breath you take in between diving off and hitting the water,
        subscribe to all the magazines in the world,
but you'll never get the hang of girls, the sullen game played
        out from summers' burnt back yards,
we need a man about this house, we need a good seeing to
        round here, a proper clean from top to bottom,
getting organised is half the battle,

sold them all a dummy today, sent them sailing into traffic
        with a flick of the hips,
smashed to pieces in my mind's eye, bones exposed beneath
        a blue sky and a red and white tape around the scene,
you don't know what I'm on about cos you've never seen it, a
        chemist shop, above the parade, sweating indoors,
curtains closed, a prescription on a dirty glass coffee table,
        you could start a fire with a magnifying glass, a ship's
        compass spinning round,
spinning fast ...

all kinds of weather we're having today, I tricked the sky into
        hysterics, weeping buckets,

wiping away the clouds with gales of laughter,
it was a glorious thunderstorm, we cried with laughter
till we couldn't see,
the wine-dark sea and me.

TAK PROMIN

I met Tony round at Marce and Mick's
one night after the pub.
It was summer time,
which I later found out
was his favourite time;
the way sunlight smashed the treetops in Pearson Park
when you slipped in off Park Grove
and you'd get that sudden flashbulb in the eyes
like the leaves had all exploded,
but anyway,
this was night-time and we'd lit up long past dark
and Tony was telling us about Bohemia,
how he'd lived in Prague.
Ey, I lived in Prague, I told him, whereabouts were you?
This was nineteen sixty-five, he said,
it wasn't like how it would have been for you.
Yeah, and how would you know?
(sparking up and kicking back, ruffling up the feathers,
a laid-back slouch attack)
I was young and full of piss and Tony's hair was white
like ash tapped from a burning spliff,
a roof weighed down with snow.
What could this old fool teach me about the wastrel life?
So we had a Boho face-off over cigarettes and wine
and Mick's black cat snaked round the floor
like a surly slice of night
as we sewed wings upon our tales
and let them all take drunken flight.
I'd had a beer with Iggy's drummer in the Marquis De Sade,
Tony checkmated Vaclav Havel
on the Golden Horse Boulevard.
I'd slept all night on Kafka's grave
with a bottle of green fairies.

Tony stopped a Russian tank
with a bouquet of white roses
and a basket of canaries.
I had a Moravian fiddle player
staying weekends at my flat;
but Tony had kissed Ivana Trump,
and I could not compete with that.
So the night went on and the talk went round
of all the books we'd read
And all the people that we'd met
and the amazing things they'd said
and no matter what I threw at him
he'd lived it thrice before:
committed humanist – beat that.
He nailed me to the floor.
And then we got a taxi
and I was skint, so he crashed for that.
And I never saw Tony to pay him back
but his name came up again
when I heard about his passing
through a friend of a friend of a friend
and that night I slept on Mick and Marcie's couch
like a hundred times before,
and when they came back off holiday
I told them: Tony's gone.
My best friend Tony,
who I met the once before.

APRICITY

Golden hour at 159, the back yard,
the stubbed out embers of the day.
The tribes of KUH are cooling down,
that ball of fire fading,
the shadow of the basketball hoop
makes a halo on the ground,
plastic nerf guns melted
in a multi-coloured pool,
a radio murmurs two gardens down,
The Isley Brothers, that bumble bee guitar,
distant, another country.

Somewhere along the ten-foot
a football bangs a garage door.
It's 4pm in the universe
and I no longer care about cholesterol levels
or the government;
the soul detaches and floats upwards,
heat rising.

That pigeon again, a sudden dart to the rooftops,
settles on the chimney, cock-eyed, leaning,
as the police helicopter above him
buzzes through blue,
an angry metal dragonfly
following the vapour trail
back to the mothership, back to the source.

Boy racers tearing up and down the avenue
and the brown and black
and pink flowers erupting,
the red necks in the beer gardens
sinking pints of amber,
the last drop of the afternoon

getting ready for the night.

The festival in the park is packing up its tents;
a giant struggles to his feet and falls back down again,
no more music leaking through the windows
or drifting down the street,
the Drum Club near the bandstand
meets monthly – all invited, all intact.

I feel the rhythm from my back yard,
but I'm too petrified to move.
I'm burnt red raw,
beads of water on glass,
a galleon afloat among the icebergs,
I've got a head full of pollen
and these bones are melting in the heat.

I traded all my earthly worries
for a doctor's note
and a mouth full of dust;
summer will be gone soon,
and these golden hours
will turn to rust.

(NOT ANOTHER) URBAN MYSTIC

Oh no, not another urban mystic
spouting hippy dippy code words
stuck together with Pritt Stick,
not another piece of sage advice
handed down from the ancient heads,
we've heard those mantras for time, man,
time to put them all to bed.
A late night audience, rings of smoke,
classic album covers
and casual weekend lovers,
good night god bless to Vishnu and Krishna
the groovy prophets from the magical east,
all them books on the shelf
stuck on page three;
the true confessions of a fraudulent priest.
Winter mornings wasted
lounging about in bed,
your mam and dad are liberals
they survived the 90's and acid house
they've seen the lot, they've seen it all,
they don't say a dicky bird
when the headboard bangs on their bedroom wall –
is your friend staying another night love?
Is there anything you need at all?
have you got some protection?
are you keeping yourself clean?
Licked spotless from arsehole to breakfast time,
we'll have both your dinners on the table for nine
on the dot, is he a vegetarian?
What does his dad do?
Any chance of you dragging yourself down

them dancers before two?
It's not an hotel, we're not your servants
Is he some sort of piss take merchant?

I wish I was twenty one again,
I wouldn't fuck about
I'd get straight on that plane to America,
drink the great lakes dry,
spread meself about like a plague,
give 'em all the glad eye,
look at him, fast asleep,
laid out like a shilling dinner,
I work these fingers down to stubs,
he's like a little fat piggy wrapped up in a blanket
and I'm only getting thinner,
that coat's seen better days, a cadaver in a shroud
it shouldn't be allowed
and I have to sit here and listen to him
pontificate in my kitchen;
the moon landings, the third eye, the secret temples of power
fucks sake, will you listen to him
harping on for hours and hours and hours,
yes mate, I remember my first microdot
left me burnt out, jaded, gone to pot.
Not another urban mystic
spouting hippy dippy code words
stuck together with Pritt Stick,
not another piece of sage advice
handed down from the ancient heads,
we've heard those mantras for time, man,
time to put them all to bed.

DRIVING AT NIGHT

One night
at 3am
I got out of bed
and into my car,
drove off
to nowhere
in particular,
just pressing pedals,
turning my hands.

No music on,
no background noise,
just lights
and white lines
and everything
the other side
of the glass
carved
out of black.

It must have been
a dream
that woke me,
a nightmare,
but that
had gone now,
the raw terror
subsiding,

its shape
hung behind me
like a bed sheet,
on the back of a door
like a ghost
on the road,
retreating.

ARTHUR

Arthur bounces out the big house
with a bag of dirty washing
and a head full of ideas,
the gap between his ears packed with visions
borne of long hours and days and weeks
and months spent horizontal,
eyes fixed on the same dissected square of grey,
an immovable masterpiece, a painting on the wall,
the laughing cavalier of the last three thousand days
but anyway, the point is, Arthur can walk unhindered
for the first time in years, no longer leaning on landings
or stopping dead at slabs of metal.

The forty odd quid burning a hole in his sky rocket,
visions of the alehouse, a can or two at least,
some proper cigs,
but have you seen the price of this?
No job, no wife, no proper digs
and the traffic is fast
the traffic is much too fast, hurtling past,
a ton of metal and glass,
a rocket fired through a restricted space,
the mighty killer whale, the black fish
killed two men, but what would you do
if you were fenced in 24 / 7 and prodded with a stick?
Welcome to the brand new bedlam
with no shortage of lunatics.

Arthur parks himself down in the nearest greasy spoon
and fills his guts with salt and hot sweet tea,
the papers spread out, half naked pop stars
and liars in suits, the cutlery like dumbbells in his hands,
scraping on the plate, the radio is playing a tune
he remembers from a previous life,

something solid back there, a monument erected,
an ancient scab peeled back and re-infected;
musicians are just like builders
but with trumpets and pianos
instead of lathes and hammers;
Sad Sweet Dreamer, bring your love back to me.

And this is about half ten and the appointment at the shelter
is not while three and there is no-one to stop him
getting up and walking through the door,
but it's safe in here, cosy, warm;
outside, it starts to hammer down with rain,
the radio playing that same chorus
again and again and again,
a shotgun blast from the past and the urge is very strong,
time to move, opening time, the pub, the first pint at
        dinnertime,
it's going in, it's gonna make his head swim,
halfway down the glass and the room is tilting sideways,
his first instinct is to spew, but he holds his breath
and the greasy grey skies of the storm pass overhead,
he opens his lungs and breathes in,
the clouds part and clean golden light pours in;
trumpets, choirs, rainbows, wings, no more second guessing
no more forms to fill in,
a guardian angel issued by the home office;
Your Majesty, Your Majesty,
I promise to keep my promise,
turn the other cheek, when in doubt, retreat,
observe the curfew closely throughout the week,
put the blinkers on, keep focused on what lies ahead,
but he's got black fingernails this cunt, can't even
keep himself clean, how's he gonna keep a house in order,
how can he mean what he says, you can't move in that
hotel for drugs, and all the rest of them monsters,
you can't wipe away the sins of the world

if you can't even wash your hands;
pissed on one pint, Arthur thinks he's died
and gone to heaven, he's got a head full of visions
and a bag full of dirty washing.

Arthur told me once, he told me the reason
he got into gear was that it made his pupils
shrink to pinpoints; he'd read somewhere
that the eyes were the window to the soul,
said he didn't want anyone
looking into his soul,
that's what Arthur told me,
goodnight god bless, no more pain,
anchor safely down,
goodnight god bless,
Arthur's home again.

CHIEF

The Chief has been my constant,
my fireplace sentry,
carved and still and stoic,
hand-hooded eyes
scoping the horizon
for some distant unseen prize.
On the Wild West prairies
of Coltman Street and Clumber Street,
The Boulevard and Newland Ave,
that summer on Convent Court;
wherever I have laid my hat
the Chief has held the fort.
A calming presence,
always gladly felt
through the days and nights of mayhem,
through wine slung rows
and smoke signals that spelt
HELP, HELP ME, PLEASE SEND HELP,
and still he stood tall
when help did not come,
a totem, a touchstone
with feathers and drum.
My silent sidekick;
the nearest I've got
to my father's other son.

FAIR DOG

He's locked outside, it's hard to make yourself heard
when there's a blanket wrapped around your head,
hard to decide the best way to stay alive
when the general consensus is you're already dead.
He picks stuff out of bins, he don't know where he's been,
the last ten weeks are a blur.
It's hard to know which way a body should go
when a body is in need of some care.

Fair dog,
dog from a fair.
Fair dog,
dog from a travelling fair.

That woman in the white coat and headphones,
she nearly always stops to stroke his back,
it's hard to know when to curl up and lie down,
when to bare your teeth and attack.
He picks stuff out of bins, he doesn't know where he's been
the last ten weeks are a blur,
he doesn't know where he is
or how he ended up there.

Fair dog,
dog from a fair.
Fair dog,
dog from a travelling fair.

DEAN LICKED MY BALLS

The words installed within me
a deep unease:
DEAN LICKED MY BALLS
four foot high in white
beneath the underpass.

I was eight years old
and driving from
the backseat of the car
going to pick up my Dad
from work.

A brush and emulsion job,
white lines running down the wall
and blurring quick
as the words loomed past:
DEAN LICKED MY BALLS

I don't think it was the imagined act
as such
as much as the setting
that unsettled me –
the underpass was a violent mess
of mattresses and broken wood
and broken glass
and broken blood
and broken dark spots
where things would possibly happen
if they possibly could.

Of course, Dean
could have had his balls licked
in the comfort of his own home,
but there was another worry upon me –
whoever wrote this,

was it a boast?
Or an exorcism in public
of a very private ghost?

I felt almost afraid to ask.
When you're eight years old
you start to know
that grown ups
sometimes
wear a mask.

I CAN SEE THE LIGHTS

Let's get you home Dad, let's get you off,
it's late and you're pissed, the time bell's been rung
and you've already missed Match Of The Day
and the last bus home,
we'll have to brave the late night streets
and you're not walking on your own,
stepping and swaying and avoiding the wars
spilling out of the alehouse doors,
these young bucks, they can't hold their drink
they can barely tie their own laces, the places
I've been, the things I've seen, sailed three times round
the world before they'd even got out their high chairs
alright, alright, calm down mister,
no need to get the dukes up,
no need to rant and curse
you don't have to take on the universe,
there's a full fat moon hanging up there,
let me take your arm and guide you past the take-aways,
under the orange sodium glow, let's talk about City,
the lads in amber and black, let's walk a staggered tango
quick quick slow,
three steps sideways
two steps back,
ignore the youth with their swagger and slurs, the streets
are full of beasts and their portable feasts, let's talk about
your glorious past; Jackie Smith and that scrob
in Kevin Ballroom, 1957, you took him down hard and fast:
quick square blow to the solar plexus,
never spilled a drop, different breed back then
yeah Dad I know, I know,
a square go, boxed off,
ten kits of cat on the quayside,
bobbers clogs striking sparks from the cobbles

22

but the dock has run dry now
the dock has run dry
... and them cowards on the telly, dressed up like tarts
I'd go over there and fight em meself, if I still had me health
half a dozen kids from Gillet street
would sort them bastards out,
what a shame about them bains, if I still had me health,
If I still had me health, I'd gladly pull the lever meself,
World's gone mad son, world's gone mad
and him off the news,
he never alters,
and my head has now detached and it's a child's balloon
        floating over the rooftops,
bumping up against
the full fat moon...
A&E will be packed to the rafters tonight
they'll be slotting em in sideways that's half the problem
none of these bastards can fight
yeah alright
alright yeah yeah yeah alright alright ...
Let's get you home Dad, let's steer by the stars,
Neptune will guide us past the iron clad shops
and shut-down bars, the bus-stop snogs,
tonight's Sports Mail, City drew away at Port Vale,
the top deck of the sixty-six,
I could walk for hours and days and months
when the memories come fast and thick,
like our house at Christmas,
festooned with lights and glitter,
you said it was just for the bains
but you can't kid a kidder
and it's almost like you're with me
walking home from pub
never take off your coat and tie when the fists start to fly,
the coppers always slap the cuffs on the man without a jacket,
the police always come too bastard late to stop it ...

... keep walking Dad, home is in sight,
I can see the lights,
I can see the lights,
I can see the lights.

LONG TIME

Seems like only yesterday when you stole the very best of me,
or was it just a year or so before?
When we stayed up all night, bathed in floods of black and
          white.
I can't remember a time since, when I felt so pure and clear,
Can't recall a day since you left
that I've woke up once without that crawling fear.

Me and you, an attic flat, a libro shirt, a junk shop hat,
or was it just a shadow on the bed?
When we rattled the windows and woke up the neighbours.
We never ate a square meal and we never felt the cold,
I felt your presence on Infirmary roof,
I saw you smiling down on me in the sky above Anlaby Road.

You can't go back, you can't go back, you can't avoid a heart
          attack
if your heart has got a knife held to your throat.
Take this chain son, may it serve you well,
wear it proud round your Beverley Beck,
I felt your presence in the bathroom when I brushed my teeth,
woke up in a sweat,
all hands on deck,
all hands on deck.

JOHNNY ROCKHEAD

Johnny schooled me just today,
cavemen never lived in caves,
killing just to burn the bones,
burn the bones to make our homes
designer temples made of tusks,
brand new homes from burnt out husks,
Johnny schooled me just today,
cavemen never lived in caves.

Dots and lines and symbols deep, painted up while we're
        asleep,
emblazoned on a garage door,
spread your fat wings, start to soar
from half past primitive to now o'clock,
Johnny Rockhead, HU9,
rocks around the block.

Stink of paint and hiss of tongues,
patch of gold and yards of green
places where my name is known,
places where I've never been
but trust me, it's there,
trust me, it's there,
I crawl down into caves
where I can't be seen.

Gotta hunt for food,
keep the family warm,
don't hunt for fun, don't kill for kicks
outside the front door,
I kill to burn the bones stark clean,
a temple, red, gold and green,
stick men chasing tigers,
close your eyes, it's engraved

modern day hard drive,
we're still enslaved
from half past now to then o'clock
Johnny Rockhead, HU9
rocks around the block.

Shamen gene, survived intact
through centuries of war,
human weakness as a matter of fact
screaming hollow pit of nowt
plummet down,
years flash by like office blocks,
a darkened shaft,
neon numbers falling
as we crash and burn and smash,
crack our heads upon the hard ground floor,
Johnny Rockhead drags himself out his pit
at half past four,
grabs his gun, work to do,
tigers to chase,
summons his nerve, head daubed in clay,
an armful of slings and shots,
red, gold and green,
crawl down in the cave –
paint your name where it can't be seen.

Drag him from his primeval pit,
Johnny Rockhead, in a bit
send him through the centuries
to where his skills best fit,
Johnny Rockhead, HU9;
evolution cannot touch me
and the gods they all love me.
Johnny schooled me just today,
caveman never live in caves.

LOLLY STICK STUCK IN SLOT CAUSES CASCADE OF COPPER

Strolling past a phone box
that suddenly erupts
with unprecedented clamour,
puncturing a slow summer afternoon
with the possibility of drama;
a wrong number, surely, a misplaced
finger, a digit missing, I mean,
who uses these cream
coloured coffins
for anything other than drug deals or pissing?
Well, how can you resist?
Step inside and lift the speaker
from the cradle,
yes?
who's this?
who's that?
I asked first,
Well I asked second
listen, pal,
I'm just a passing citizen
who reckoned
that passing by a ringing box
would be akin to ignoring
a cry for aid;
some kidnapped victim perhaps
bound in a chair, temporarily unengaged,
handset held to mouth, one false word
and they're dead,

or an isolated pensioner
aching for a human voice
from some distant corner of the map,
but then again,
it could be a trap;
the last time you were in one of these
a lolly stick stuck in a slot
caused a cascade of copper,
but now you could be
caught in the crosshair of a lurking
rooftop sniper,
your brains about to decorate the squares of glass
with a sudden explosion of red,
a fresh interior paint job,
your last conscious thought
left unrecorded,
as the line
goes dead.

MAYFAIR

All day breakfast plate piled up opposite the Pentonville
     panopticon,
that's where they stick you if you can't behave,
a twelve by eight foot concrete grave,
me and Bob The Artist at 8 am
scraping our plates with the rest of the working men
and women with whistles and locks and keys
fastened on chains hung down by their knees.
A million hash browns later
we're cradling our bellies down the road to Kings Cross.

Is this your favourite part of London?
Bob shows me forgotten corners;
Edwardian poet's residence and letters home from young
     offenders,
you can't smoke more than four foot from a bar,
there's lines on the pavements so you know exactly where you
     are,
Camden Borough Council dictate where you can stand
and the angle of your cigarette
as it dangles from your hand.
Bob the artist's got a sporran on
cos in London nobody cares what you got up your skirt,
nobody's bothered about your love bites or bruises
or your ballads of urban hurt.

We're led into a room and surely some mistake,
there's balconies over courtyards and cut glass fountains
and lakes of booze
and Bob's nudging me in the back, whispering
play it cool man just play it cool –
adopt a weary hipster pose, like you've seen it all before
like you're bored off your arse with Cuban jazz
and Mexican Bloody Marys,

you can't take any more, they only make you thirsty
they only make your cracked lips sore
so we duck out double quick,
start dishing out cards round Soho.
Bobs making an exhibition of himself,
those breakfasts don't pay for themselves you know,
two easels at once
with Gil Scott-Heron on the decks,
them London afternoons just fly by man
when you're flying by the seat of your kegs.

MONDAY MORNING, 10am

used to have wallpaper with
racing cars and a lampshade,
a fringe on the bottom

mattress on the floor of
a child's bedroom
and a grown up, forgotten

plans lost in the fog and
scabs like red jewels,
teeth black and rotten

voices on the radio,
music in another room,
yellow sheets sodden

stain on the barrel and
drops of brown rust on the
white ball of cotton

OFF TO BEER-OFF

I'm off to beer-off, d'yer want out? I'm off to beer-off in a bit. If yer want owt getting write us a list if yer want cigs or skins or goodies or milk or a bottle of plonk, a few cans, some vodka, a box of matches, a note from the doctor saying please let me stay in bed for a week I've been drinking for ten days flat and now I can't speak so write down your list while I'm getting me coat, have a good think about what your heart needs the most, a treehouse, a rocket, a place in the sun, a gold mine, an extended lifetime, get me a bag for life pass me a kitchen knife, I'm off to beer-off, d'yer want out?

I'm off to beer-off, d'yer want out? I'm off to off beer-off after this, for a blast of cold air, and one off the Oliver Twist, a siren, a signal, an eighteen-carat diamond dropped on the deck, digging for treasure in the snow – someone fell down a gap in the system down there – mind how you go. I know a shortcut down a ten-foot, there's a handy mattress if you need a quick lie down – there's a fine layer of powder on the ground and everything looks pale blue and beautiful under this light – sharp shadows loom in me peripheries, I forgot the list, I can't tell me left from me right, I'll strike out into the cold dark night – I'm off to beer-off, d'yer want out?

I'm off to beer-off, d'yer want out? I'm off to beer-off real soon. I'm not frightened of clowns or kids on paper rounds or Herbert Sherbet with his bag of kali. I'm gonna rinse the till when she reaches for the wine gonna take back what's rightfully mine all them nights passing over chunks of corn for sorrowful mornings after joyful nights, May the dark gods of Boulevard forgive me, even sullen eyed vampires deserve their semi-human rights, there's things out there you would not believe, pass me a kitchen knife to slide up me sleeve, I'm getting wrapped up, it's bitter out, I'm off to beer-off, d'yer want out?

BENEATH THE FLYOVER, SUMMER '82

Y cardies and wedges,
finger and flick,
bleached and bobbing
like a nervous tic,
lurked beneath the flyover
with tubes of Evo-Stik.

Summer saw a multitude
of sniffers, psychos, skins,
floating skulls
with eyes like pins
gathered in the evening gloom
with plastic bags and tins,

chased by giant Mars Bars,
glow electric green
through crackling fields of pylons,
barely in their teens;
back of a jam sandwich,
glue stains on their jeans.

Spots and sores and red raw rash,
blowtorch breath and scabs,
ice-cold blast of butane,
twenty stolen tabs,
shaking like a shitting dog,
lungs like frozen glass.

Y cardies and wedges,
finger and flick,
bleached and bobbing
like a nervous tic

lurked beneath the flyover
with tubes of Evo-Stik.

EART'S SUPPOSED TO
LAST

It was hotter than that summer in the seventies
when the ladybirds swarmed the washing
and the sun was blinding white
and our mouths were alive with lemonade lollies
and the council stopped the water fights
I'd been telling them all about this how it was a
long time before they were born
but it was too warm for bedtime
and they were both starting to yawn
so we started chasing each other
round the kitchen to I Fought The Law
them two with plastic swords
me with my invisible guitar
round and round the room we ran then
we stopped, breathless, and they said:
can you feel our hearts Dad?
If it stops does it mean that you're dead?
I put fingers to each bony ribcage
and there they were, five and eight years old
tiny thump thump thump thump thumps
too late for biscuits too early for bed
can you feel mine? I said,
hands planted flat on my chest
I can't feel it, they said
well, can you hear it I said
hand cupped behind ears, grinning, taking
the mick,
no, I said, put your head on
here,
to the part that makes us tick
foreheads propped against my gut

like in prayer at the Wailing Wall
no, I said,
I mean, like you do with a sea-shell
when you hear the mermaids call.
Two heads twist and listen
four eyes widen below
can you hear it now, I say?
yeah! he said
It's really loud, she said
and proper fast!
That's good I said
cos a heart's supposed to last.

PRECIOUS FLOWER

You're such a precious flower, she said,
that job at the call centre is getting to you,
I can tell,
maybe it would be best for both of us if you packed a small
       bag,
got yourself off for a while,
go to a hotel
get a room in some big city,
someplace where your face is not known,
park yourself at a nearby bar,
live in a film for a fortnight or so,
watch aliens pass across the screen,
frame them with a single click,
capture their dreams in monochrome,
project yourself, protect yourself, don't think of home,
try not to think of me when you're twisting in sheets
under dim red light,
wring your darkest thoughts out clean,
peg them out above the bath
watch them bleed down the drain,
watch something on the telly that makes you laugh,
you should stop dwelling on the past, she said.
Do not touch the dinosaur,
do not rouse his sleeping bones
risen from the Ice Age,
the centuries cracked and peeling away,
emerging from the eggshell,
skin glistens like a newborn,
have you seen the vultures circling overhead?
hold a baby vulture in your hand
and tell me the dinosaurs are dead,
tell me we never crawled out between the cracks
of the frozen lakes of Africa after the spaceship fell

down from skies of orange flame,
pushed the start button,
fired the pistol,
set the clock hands of the centuries ticking slowly once again,
we're waiting for the golden haired angel
to bathe us in the light,
we're waiting for the spaceship to re-ignite the night,
seven years of warfare, then the peace we all deserve,
but you're such a precious flower,
they'll leave you here on earth,
you wouldn't like the universe
it's hard to fill your lungs out there,
you're such a precious flower, she said,
that job at the call centre is sending you insane,
get yourself away from telephones, she said.
get away from screens,
go and rent a cottage near the sea,
bring us back some dreams.

HULL

In the 50's
60's
and
part of
the 70's
most of the men
were away
at sea.

> Since the 80's to
> now
> most of the men
> are
> still away
> and
> some of them
> are still
> at sea.

INDUCTION

Every Monday morning I stand up
before twenty or so disinterested faces
slouched around library tables
and tell them
about the possibilities of poetry
and the prospect of escape.

It's a poor joke and some mornings
it goes down less well than others.

Like this one morning,
a sullen soul soul flinging rancour
from the back of the room:

What's that for then?
What do you get at the end of it?
Do you get paid?
So what use is that to me?

And I said,
(quoting Scargill's Dad)
The quality of your life
depends upon
your ability to manipulate words.

He thought about this
for half a second.

Does it fuck
he said,
thus proving
both
of our points.

PRISON SONG

Stark white light
in corridors of blank
and endless time
squeal with soles
that trod these paths
a thousand times before
and their joking and jeers,
heavy handed slaps.
In regulation grey and green they go,
inked-in necks and hands,
medicine eyeballs spinning slow.
A merry-go-round of men;
nothing moves in here,
the pale green walls
crumbling year by year,
the tables in the classrooms tattooed
with names and dates and cities,
football teams and slogans too,
swollen cartoon titties,
threats and symbols:
BEECHY OV OPE
JACKO IS A NONCE
a swastika, a ganja leaf,
a tumescent cock spitting tears
and, as night time descends
and the shadows
lengthen like the years,
the TVs burn themselves blank
and the banging on the pipes
the voices at the windows,
shouting sideways
up and down:
Ey mate! Give us a song!

Ey! Lad!
Yeah, you!
Next pad down,
go on, give us all a song.
And this is what he sang:
Prison stinks of bleach and sweat,
boiled up cabbage and regret,
prison stinks of wild-eyed plans,
of easy money in far off lands.
Prison stinks like seeping gas,
sleep and sympathy,
neither last.
Prison stinks of bodies packed
in tiny halls and tiny pads,
of toilet pans and burning foil,
sour milk and twice-fried oil,
laundry bags and bags of burn
and bags of time as clock hands turn.
The showers stop at half past six,
they stop your meds if you're not sick,
but tablets melt the days away
and subbie stops the drag of days.
The desperate stink of empty hours
behind the doors where bullies cower,
piss break when the screws about,
stand fast when they can't keep count,
prison stinks like an egg gone black
so take big sniffs
and don't come back.

MIRROR

What do you see?
a mark between eye and cheek
when you smile, the clouds roll back
posters on your bedroom wall,
perfect eyes and perfect hair,
perfect teeth and waist and there
lies the problem,
therein lies the lie;
a photoshopped face
is not a true reflection
it's just a perfect lie.
You don't know how beautiful you are,
powder paint conceal,
nothing is more beautiful
than something that is real.

MURDERING THE HOURS

You add them up,
the wasted hours
spent
looking out of the window,
pacing up and down
making cups of tea
that go cold
at your elbow,
flicking back the nets
at the slightest passing sound
or shadow.
And you do everything:
smoking
sulking
smarting
seething
waiting
for that
mystic moment,
doing
everything
anything
except sitting down
and doing
the thing that
you say
you want all the time in the world
to do.

REX EVERYTHING

Rex Everything came ambling past my door
No longer addicted to chocolate or pot,
no longer taking photos,
he sat in my kitchen and I saw
the absence in his eyes,
and remember, this is the man
who had built a papier mache monster
seven foot in size
big blue eyes and big red lips
from the pissed on wrappers of patty and chips,
who had politely asked permission
to hold up a bank
with a yellow water pistol,
(which, he assured the girl,
fired blanks)
and was later found waist deep
in despair
in a pond in the park by the police.
The man who bought a Lottery ticket every day
at 8am and pegged them out
on a washing line,
one by one,
Monday next to Tuesday,
and so on, and then,
at five to eight on a Saturday night,
doused them all with Zippo fluid
and set his week of hope aflame
in one swift amber whoosh,
capture it on camera
and then slow it down
frame by frame
into a potentially award winning short film
called "Over By Sunday",

that never got made,
due to mass indifference
and a lack of Lottery Funding.

Rex said,
I'm writing poetry now
but I've had a few problems.
How so?
Well, for instance, I'll think
I know,
I'll write a poem about the world
But then I'll think of the world
and the actual word world
and then I'll think:
what other thing rhymes with the world?
And he looked at me:
Well, what about furled?
Furled?
Yeah, furled;
as in the opposite of unfurled,
as in like a flag.
He looked at me, considered.
Is that even a word?
But he wrote it down, glad:
furled
a grin of delight on his face that abruptly
gave way
to sudden wounded
despair,
a face
so utterly bereft and
sad.
Yeah, he said,
That's all well and good,
but what comes
after that?

SHADOW WILL NOT WALK WITH ME

My shadow will not walk with me,
he trails ten paces behind.
I try to trick him sometimes
by stopping at a shop display
and eyeing up the goods
but he hangs back, blends in
keeps out of the way,
no matter where the sun
is settled in the sky
he's cut free from my ankles,
keeps a sullen distance,
trailing through the streets
like a two-bit private eye.
Parks and open space and green
offer no encouragement;
a disobedient dog is he,
skulking by the fringe of trees.
I am incomplete without him;
my personal penumbra,
my two dimensional brother
slipping like water over kerbstones
and red brick walls and wrought iron railings,
my half brother in waiting.
When I get home he's hiding
somewhere in some shady corner,
scurries from the sudden snap of
electric white light, the indoor sun flicked on
banishes him like a cockroach –
there and there and there and
then gone.
No dogs' heads or doves' wings

made with fingers
fluttering on the bedroom wall.
My shadow will not talk to me,
like I'm not there at all.

RIME

BLACK CLOUD

Get that down yer man we've time for one more quick un,
make it a lager with a little gold 'un on the side,
just enough to steel yourself over the outgoing tide,
it's rough as arseholes out there tonight, get a glow inside yer,
we'll be alright kid, the old man knows his stuff,
a steady hand in the wheelhouse as we bid goodbye to the
        land,
when the sky is black and all lit up the sea is rough.
Shut up about your lass and all that Saner Street carry on,
the dead can't talk man, they're finished, they're gone, they're
        gone.
Fretting like a tart, look at Dillinger, spragged from nearly
        every firm,
he's not arsed, been on walkabout for three month now,
the devil will make work,
he swapped all the bains round in their prams outside Coin-
        Op,
I'm telling yer man it's true, your lass and their Carol
were that busy yapping they dint notice till they got home,
        mind you,
I can't sail with Dill anymore, it all gets too much,
heard all his repartee before, clever cunt, the same old gags,
the same old one-man show,
putting the fear of Christ into all the deckie learners,
gerrem in a daisy chain, that'll bastard learn em,
anyway, c'mon brother, finish that drop, the bell's about to
        go,
yeah I know mate, this is the last trip you're doing,
I know, I know, I know,
you're chucking it after this, I hear what you're saying my
        brother,

there must be more to life than this, more than ice and sea
            and fish.
I'm the same, I'm gonna be an astronaut, work me ticket to
            the stars,
get a house out in the sticks, a brand new motor car,
but in the meantime we need to feed all them bains
that you keep knocking out,
keep everyone at home in the manner they're accustomed,
Christmas has cleaned you out,
but no one on that road will go without,
so take off yer band of gold, before the gates get unlocked,
shake the salt out your bag and get yerself on dock. . .

... but he can't get it out of his head, what she said,
their lass, that Mrs Hudson down Saner Street,
three nights before last:
Keep your men at home girls, don't let them go back to sea –

A black cloud's gonna cover this city
not one, not two, but three,
a black clouds gonna cover this city,
not one, not two, but three.

ICEBERG IN THE GUTS

Steaming out about 14 knots,
an ant on the back of a whale
five days from deep water,
all that wind and shite and hail
bunked up below the whaleback,
A dime store cowboy paperback,
it's the last chance I'll get
to chase Indians across a plain,
the last chance I'll get
before the horizontal rain
and the red raw hands
and no feet beneath

face lashed by nails,
Christmas crackers, a half-price sale.
There's a fella in Kirkella
with blood on his hands,
We are an ant on the back of a whale.

Shoot
Shoot

eighteen hours non-stop graft
where's there's ice there's cash,
north of the Arctic Circle,
breeding season on the continental shelf,
silver fat-bellied clouds bursting underwater
food for hungry sons and daughters,
shoals of silver babies wriggling through the nets,
shoals of silver mams and dads
dragged gasping on the deck,
a vision in me head
and the cold hard slap face of reality,
sea comes on board
and salt scrapes out your eyes and the inside of your skull,
wind, waves,
there's a woman sat down Saner Street sobbing,
visions of untended graves,
she's an ant on the back of a whale

Shoot
Shoot

I think of our lass
at home by the fire,
a seed in her belly,
put there by me,
a feeling,
a father, a mother,
a three-day millionaire,
full time provider, part time lover,

left it there
a hope,
some kind of insurance
and the nail gun in the side of my head
an iceberg in my guts.
nine tenths waiting on the outgoing tide
and I can hear the ghosts of Saner Street
screaming in the wind on the starboard side

Shoot
Trawl
Guts
Freeze

SING OUR SOULS TO SLEEP

If I should wake up in my sleep
roll me over
roll me over.
Lay me down to sleep,
lift these troubles from my eyes
lay me down to sleep.
If I'm roused up from my bed
lay me over
lay me over,
send me safe to bed.
Roll the clouds from low above
send me down to sleep,
if the Mission man comes round your house
send me over
send me over,
send me back to sleep.
Call our people home again,
sing our souls to sleep.
Lay me over,
send me home,
send our love across the airwaves

Sing our souls to sleep
Sing our souls to sleep
Sing our souls to sleep.

HOME

Hey Rowland!
Get on that VHF
send word to our lass
get me suit out of Turners
get your best frock on
tell em in Halfway
tell em in Rayners . . .

We're steering by the stars above,
we're rising up through rime and foam
we're steering by the light of love,
we're coming home
we're coming home.

No more will I leave the land,
no longer will I roam
kiss the bains goodnight god bless,
we're coming home
we're coming home.

Three ships of ghosts
back from the storm,
we're coming home
we're coming home.

Men of stars,
ancient bones
we're coming home
we're coming home.

The sea is cold,
hearts are warm

we're coming home
we're coming home.

Deckie Learner
you're coming home,
Chief Engineer
you're coming home,
Bosun
you're coming home,
Cook
you're coming home,
Spare Hand
you're coming home,
Trimmer
you're coming home,
Mate
you're coming home,
Wireless Operator
you're coming home,
Skipper
you're coming home,
Second Engineer
you're coming home,
Third Hand
you're coming home,
Spare Hand
you're coming home,
You're coming home.

The sirens sing me to sleep.

OWFLAKES

It hits you hardest
when you least expect,
like a Christmas choir
on a website at work
in the middle of July

the silent snow
falling,
heaped up on the screen
then spectral voices
rising

and you think about
that thing,
the thing that happened
and is still happening
and won't stop happening
and how Christmas
is fucked forever
now

and you feel your eyes pricking,
the sun
pressing at the window,
the choir
still singing
in your head,

piano and strings,
the world's smallest violin
and snowflakes falling,
hitting the desk
at 10.32 am.

SPIDERMAN UNMASKED

You fell off the back of a lorry with a coil of blue rope,
a mobile phone, a phrase book, a passport
that you bought off a bloke;
the photo don't look nothing like you,
but it don't matter to the people,
they look right through you,
they only know the faces they clock on TV
when they're face down and silent
and washed up by the sea
but that's not thee, you're safe and sound,
set down on dry land and you melt into the city,
lose yourself in the heat and the noise
and the back to back buildings,
the sellotaped names described under doorbells,
blankets up for nets, lines of indoor washing,
rows of mobile phones on charge
and the beds on heavy rotation,
the mattress don't get a chance to get cold,
stacked up by the landlords, they're dragged off the skips,
ten to a room, twelve hour shifts,
up to the hips in cake mix
up to the eyeballs in giblets,
morning shift, double back shift,
sick to your stomach on chicken blood and shit
and you come home exhausted but you're happy and glad
no one's firing guns and the bad things are behind you,
dripping down, all the juice drained
out of a tangerine sun.

Then a man said he knows a man
whose cousin got a start with Deep Pan Pete,
delivering pizzas after dark;
a moped and a luminous vest;

the money's not great but it's the best you can get
and it's a start, it's a step and they could do with a hand,
you're on the yellow brick road to the promised land,
no more chicken giblets, no more puddles of blood,
there's a non-stop demand for carbohydrates
and plastic cheese and warm bread in trays
and salad and dips and strips of sweaty meat,
so you put on the gear and rev up the ride
with a sock full of loose change
and a box full of heat,
but you don't know the drill and you don't know the streets,
you don't know how to carry on
when the food is snatched from your hand
and the door gets slammed –
there's some minor drama going off every night,
always someone rowing and wanting a fight
and your nerves are all shot and you come off the bike.

New identity must be found, they sack you off the round
but give you one last chance,
the bright spark son of the boss
who treats you like a cunt, has a brilliant idea,
a genius stunt – he gets the outfit together
from an internet site, gets a sign knocked up
and you're magically transformed,
the public face of Deep Pan Pete:
Spiderman by the side of the road,
stop me and buy one,
stop now and try one,
get out of that kitchen and scatter those pots and pans,
treat yourself at Deep Pan Pete's,
courtesy of your friendly neighbourhood Spiderman.

And it's hot beneath the mask, but it's cash in hand
and the mobile credit runs out faster than sand
through your hands and you wave to the kids
in the back of the cars and some wave back

58

and that makes you feel grand;
secret identity, man of mystery,
a scourge or a saviour
and if you could read what the papers say about you
you'd piss yourself laughing at the fairy tales they peddle,
chasing swans in the park,
selling tabs under the counter after dark
but you know how it works:
people ring up home and they say, there's work here,
there's work to do,
they're ravaged by war
and attacked by villains,
they need superheroes on the street,
they don't eat proper food
they don't look after themselves,
they force feed their kids with trays full of shit
and the kids stop waving
and your arms held up in surrender finally drop
and you head back to the shop

and you peel off your face and say fuck it,
I quit,
stick this sign up your arse
and the bright spark son shrugs
and he laughs
and then he's sparked out on the deck,
he's on his back.

You've discovered your secret powers, man.
Spiderman unmasked.

YOUR SISTER IN SACREMENTO

The night watchman has fallen asleep on his watch,
scene from a porno frozen on his laptop
and a half supped bottle of scotch;
you tiptoe past him in the dark blue of the dawn,
punch your password into your machine,
email your sister in Sacramento
saying send us some dough, I can't take this anymore,
these grey concrete dawns and glass-fronted boxes
they're squeezing my dreams,
cutting short my nights,
I'm in work at half three in the AM
well, it's nearly four
and four is nearly five,
I have to spark one up just to get me in here,
the eyes of the building open one by one
winking yellow windows
one by steady one,
money's getting tight –
I've stretched it way past snapping point,
every day is the same,
it feels like aimless wandering down silent dead end lanes
the streets are full of shops with the Christmas lights on
but nobody's buying nothing,
the shelves are collapsing,
there's a tailback from town,
the streets are wet and orange
all headlights dipped
and a lad in a uniform sits drooling at a screen,
he can't make up his mind if what he's watching
is decent or obscene,
he can't make much sense of the suffering he has seen

or maybe that is just a conceit,
maybe he is merely the keeper of the gate
and not the guardian of all we know,
maybe he's not letting on as much as I think he should
      although
what with me being his chief spokesman on earth
at least that is what we are led to believe;
that you are the author of all creation,
he is not equipped to enter into such hunger games,
Christ, what worlds these punters have at their fingertips,
what frames of reference waiting to be filled – fuck me
I should knock this AM smoke on the head,
anyway,
you should see the view from up here;
a house with blue windows, blue light behind glass
lit up like a chocolate box,
like a 70's TV advert when Christmas was golden.
See the face you love light up, remember that?

SEND

Your sister in Sacramento must be out
Time difference, no doubt
The guard is mumbling, roused by foxes rooting through the
      bins
The workers are coming in
The workers are coming in
The workers are coming in.

61

THE HARPIC BROTHERS

The Harpic Brothers are clean round the bend,
they live in a house at the end
of our street, with a kitchen full of chip fat
and a garden full of rust,
a mam on medication
who they wheel down to the pub.
Albert's the one with the gravestone teeth
and hair that stands up
like a cartoon cat on heat.
Trevor is the brains of the team,
his tattoos all spelt right.
They patrol the local neighbourhood
in the pitch black still of night
singing at the full fat moon
until the first damp crack of light
spills it's milky residue
over pavements, parks and streets
and the Harpics stagger home to bed,
beat a temporary retreat
from a world that slings its barbs and sneers
from passing cars and kids
on mountain bikes who batter doors
and clatter dustbin lids,
hatred is passed from parent down
to offspring like a gift.
Albert plays Dean Martin
to send his mam to sleep,
Trevor stands guard with a cricket bat,
their castle walls to keep
free of interlopers,
free from prying eyes
as his brother and their mother
sleep safely side by side.

Acknowledgements

Love and deepest respect to Tracey and Phil and everyone at Wild Pressed Books.

Big love to all the poets of the planet.

Lightning Source UK Ltd.
Milton Keynes UK
UKHW041303160220
358799UK00001B/36